D0354208

NO LONGER PROPERTY OF
SEATTLE PUBLIC LIBRARY

· NORTHWEST ·
KNOW-HOW

BEER

· NORTHWEST ·
KNOW-HOW

BEER

Jacob Uitti

Illustrations by **Jake Stoumbos**

SASQUATCH BOOKS
SEATTLE

Copyright © 2021 by Sasquatch Books

All rights reserved. No portion of this book may be reproduced or
utilized in any form, or by any electronic, mechanical, or other means,
without the prior written permission of the publisher.

Printed in China

SASQUATCH BOOKS with colophon is a registered trademark
of Penguin Random House LLC

25 24 23 22 21   9 8 7 6 5 4 3 2 1

Text: Jacob Uitti
Illustrations: Jake Stoumbos
Editor: Daniel Germain
Production editor: Bridget Sweet
Designer: Alicia Terry

Library of Congress Cataloging-in-Publication Data
Names: Uitti, Jacob, author.
Title: Northwest know-how : beer / by Jacob Uitti.
Other titles: Northwest knowhow, beer
Description: Seattle : Sasquatch Books, 2021. | Series: Northwest know-how
| Includes bibliographical references and index.
Identifiers: LCCN 2020028212 | ISBN 9781632173515
Subjects: LCSH: Beer--Northwest, Pacific.
Classification: LCC TP577 .U37 2021 | DDC 663/.4209795--dc23
LC record available at https://lccn.loc.gov/2020028212

ISBN: 978-1-63217- 351-5

Sasquatch Books
1904 Third Avenue, Suite 710
Seattle, WA 98101

SasquatchBooks.com

To the taps, barstools, and 'keeps
that I'll always remember

Contents

PLUS . . .

Introduction

·PNW·

Abundance of the Northwest

Beer is one of the oldest and most popular beverages in the world. In its purest form, the recipe is simple: boil grains in hot water and then add yeast to the liquid to start fermentation. Yet, with the addition of hops for flavoring, the results are seemingly endless. There are many beer styles—such as pale ales, pilsners, hefeweizens, and porters—and each contain a multitude of varieties made from specific combinations of these few ingredients.

More than any other, the word *craft* signifies Pacific Northwest beer. The term points to both the many microbreweries between Oregon and Washington, as well as the many varieties of beer each brewery conceives of and produces. But while beer brewing is a major part of the food and drink culture in the Northwest, there isn't a specific process prominent in any given locale. This isn't like Southern barbecue, which has a distinct St. Louis style, Kansas City style, Memphis style, and the like. Rather, throughout the Northwest, variety is key.

In some parts of the world, specific recipes are tied to certain regions. Pilsners, for example, were invented in the Czech Republic. Lagers are from Germany and monks in Belgium first made Trappist ales. But throughout the Northwest, experimentation and selection remain the preeminent focus. "The Northwest is all about choice," says Larry Rock, the first brewer at the historic Maritime Pacific Brewing Company and veteran beer industry man. "You can't pin the area down to just one style."

But craft beer abundance hasn't always been the reality for the region. Prior to the 1980s, beer drinkers imbibing at their favorite taverns or local pubs consumed either cheap domestic stuff or the often-skunky European imports shipped across oceans. But that changed in 1981 when Redhook Brewery planted its flag in the Emerald City. At that time craft beer brewing was brand-new. Only two years prior, pioneer Sierra Nevada Brewing Company started releasing its pale ales in Northern California. But word traveled fast and the trend soon hit the woodsy Northwest.

Redhook's Extra Special Bitter became an early favorite in the region in the mid-80s. Seeing Redhook's quick success, other breweries started to pop up in the Northwest, including Seattle's Hart Brewing (now Pyramid Brewing Company) and Portland's Widmer Brothers Brewing in 1984, Deschutes Brewery in 1988, Pike Brewing Company in 1989, Mac & Jack's Brewery in 1993, and Elysian Brewing Company in 1995. Over the decades, the beer culture has grown in the region from one or two pioneers to include hundreds of breweries trying to home in on the moment's premier recipe.

Today craft beer connoisseurs in the region can buy cans in barbershops while they wait for a trim or fill glass growlers with a variety of specialty ales to go at their corner drug store. To wit, almost every restaurant has craft beer in bottles or on tap, and the same goes for sports stadiums, theaters, and concert venues, which used to be the uncontested domain of mega-brew monoliths. To fill this large demand, breweries produce batch after batch for curious customers, creating oddities such as peanut butter stouts and jalapeño hefeweizens to go with their beloved IPAs and lagers.

In the global marketplace there aren't many fields where collaboration between competitors is the norm, but in the Northwest breweries often work together. Oregon's Fort George Brewery, for example, releases an annual 3-Way IPA in conjunction with two other notable breweries each year. And Fort George cofounder Jack Harris says the region's collaborative spirit is "the single factor that has kept me interested in the industry for so long."

Charity is also a major component to the region's brewing culture. Hundreds of kegs are donated each year to local events and fundraisers from breweries between Vancouver, BC, and Portland, Oregon. And some companies, such as Georgetown Brewing Company in Seattle, take it a step further. Ever since 2005, Georgetown has raised more than $100,000 a year for local charities with its Bob's Brown Ale, named in honor of a fallen friend of the brewery's cofounder Manny Chao. Each year Bob's mother chooses which charity will receive the money.

In the nature-loving Northwest, craft beer connects beer-drinking residents to local farms and ingredients. Perhaps more than anything else, it's the abundance and quality of that simple recipe's building blocks that help brewers think up and create new varieties every day.

Variety
is
key.

Unparalleled Access

While there is no set Northwest brewing style and no specific beer signature to the region—like, say, baguettes are to Paris—breweries in the region benefit from the area's wealth of premier hops and grains and the temperate, damp climate. Together these provide the perfect conditions for brewing.

Hops, which are small green buds shaped like pine cones, have little to no use other than to flavor beer. Hops provide the floral, bitter, citrusy, grassy, or piney notes to the suds, depending on the combination used and when they are added during the brewing process.

The United States accounts for about half of the world's hop production, and Washington's Yakima Valley and Oregon's Willamette Valley produce about 90% of the country's hops each year. The only country that approaches that production is Germany, which produces about 40% of the world's hops.

Originally, brewers in the United Kingdom used what are referred to as the noble hops—Hallertau, Saaz, Spalt, and Tettnang—to brew beer. Today, though, there are many more varieties. Popular options include the citrusy Cascade, floral Centennial, piney Chinook, and fruity Mosaic. In the Yakima Valley, not only do farmers grow many of these hops varieties, but they also create new hybrids.

Hops are so crucial to the region's culture that entire festivals are devoted to their popularity. In the Yakima Valley during the late summer and early fall, local hop farmers harvest their crop and breweries rush these "fresh hops" to their facilities to brew fresh-hop IPAs (a.k.a. wet-hop IPAs). Just weeks later the breweries showcase their limited-edition citrusy brews at Yakima Valley's popular annual Fresh Hop Ale Festival, often set in October. (For a list of festivals in the region, see page 128.)

While the region is a hop haven, the Northwest is also a hub for producing brewing grains. Washington's Skagit Valley, which is some 250 miles from Yakima Valley, produces a rich variety of grains used to brew beers from hoppy IPAs to dark stouts to bright pilsners. The Skagit Valley Malting Company, the region's largest micro-malt facility, thrives. Each year the company supplies about a dozen varieties of grains to over 250 breweries, mostly along the West Coast.

Historically in Skagit Valley barley was grown as a rotation crop to improve soil health. To move the product at harvest, the stuff was sold at break-even prices. But more recently, with the rise of craft beer, companies such as Skagit Valley Malting have found new and improved uses for the grains. And because a wide supply of grains means a wide variety of beer flavor options, many brewers take advantage of their harvests.

Skagit Valley Malting, however, is not alone in their work. Other micro-malthouses such as Mecca Grade in Oregon, Great Western Malting in Washington, and about sixty others throughout the United States help to provide nuance for the craft beer brewed in America via a multitude of grains. "You can't make distinctive beer if you use the same ingredients as everyone else," says Skagit Valley Malting CEO Dave Green. Of course, he's right.

And if all these excellent ingredients weren't enough, many brewers say the water in the region is conducive to brewing and excellent for making a wide array of beer styles. "Seattle water is fairly soft and the pH fairly neutral," says Georgetown Brewing Company's Manny Chao. "That's a good place to start because it allows brewers to manipulate the water for whatever styles they want to make."

In the following pages, dear reader, you will learn about dozens of beer styles, their histories, typical alcohol content (or ABV), and characteristics, as well as the myriad beer glasses created to present those beers properly, from showcasing hue to promoting carbonation. You will also learn about the origin of beer itself, what a *crowler* and a *cicerone* are, and when your favorite beer went vegan. *Cheers!*

7,000 YEARS ≈ AGO.

AD 900

1800

Where Did Beer Come From?

Perhaps the most interesting thing about beer is that it came to us by accident. Most likely, either a farmer collecting grain in a field left a bag of it behind during a rainstorm or someone left a bowl of primitive cereal out for a week in water that mixed with wild yeasts from the air. Either way, seven thousand years ago the grains fermented and beer—our most wonderful mistake—was created.

For a long time the first known historical reference to beer was the Ninkasi poem, a nearly four-thousand-year-old Sumerian verse written in reverence to the goddess of brewing. Recently, though, pottery with beer residue was unearthed in China dating back more than one thousand years before the poem. And while bread is commonly understood to be responsible for the start of human civilization, beer has shown itself to be a major player in that conversation as well.

Many thousands of years ago beer was a source of calories for workers. It was also, because it was brewed at boiling temperatures, a source of clean drinking water. Dangerous microbes were killed off in the making of the stuff. And beer, of course, made life a bit more bearable with its signature buzz. Soon it became a reason to stop and settle (near grain fields) and later, a propellant toward establishing commerce in society.

Beer's first modern heroes were women and monks. As the Dark Ages passed and civilization began to ramp up into modernity, beer was the purview of home kitchens and monasteries. In European towns women ran the brewhouses and beer was made for family and friends, with the extras sold in taverns often connected to the home. Outside of town, monks toiled over their recipes, honing the stuff as a way of honoring God. They were the first to flavor beer with hops, around AD 900.

Fast-forward to the 1800s and the industrial revolution, which brought with it the mass production of beer. It was now made in large scale and shipped around the world, paving the way for big modern companies. In 1920 Prohibition became law, shuttering the small, women-run brewhouses. And when Prohibition lifted in 1933, most folks who had made beer locally had no money to start back up again.

This was the opening that giant beer companies needed. With all the competition gone, Anheuser-Busch, Coors, and Miller ran much of the market. But in 1978 something important changed: President Jimmy Carter signed into law the right for private citizens to home-brew. People could now legally experiment with craft beer in small batches. Four decades later, more than seven thousand craft breweries dot the United States landscape, including hundreds in the Northwest.

BEER STYLES

IN TERMS OF PROCESS, there are two significant distinctions you may hear when discussing beer: "top-fermented" ales and "bottom-fermented" lagers. For our purposes in this book, however, we will think of beer in four separate categories more relevant to those of us enjoying the finished product: ales, wheat beers, porters, and lagers.

WARM-FERMENTED

60° 75°

· ALES ·

The first beers humans ever drank were ales, rudimentary as they were. Ales, which are fermented in warm temperatures around 60-75 degrees F, use the ancient and rather ubiquitous *Saccharomyces cerevisiae* yeast and the process takes about a week. Ales are generally thicker, fruity, or citrusy, and opaque in their range of colors. Because ales have such a long history, there are many varieties made today, ranging from dark and sweet to bright and citrusy.

American Amber Ale

Brewed with amber and crystal malts, amber ales range from copper to very dark brown in color. They are brewed with fewer hops than American pale ales, and as a result the beers taste rounder, or less sharp than hoppier varieties. Historically, amber ales are sweeter, even caramelly, but recently breweries such as Double Mountain Brewery in Hood River, Oregon, have been experimenting with hopped red ales that they call India red ales. These stronger, floral, and fuller-bodied beers are a growing favorite.

AVERAGE ABV: 4.5–6%

NOTABLE LOCAL OPTIONS: Mac & Jack's African Amber (Redmond, WA), Georgetown Brewing Company Chopper's Red Ale (Seattle, WA), Maritime Pacific Brewing Company Night-watch Dark Ale (Seattle, WA), Full Sail Brewing Company Amber Ale (Hood River, OR), Central City Brewers Red Racer Amber Ale (Surrey, BC), Double Mountain Brewery IRA (Hood River, OR)

GLASSWARE: Tumbler

American Blonde Ale

Where the average American pale ale is orange in color, blonde ales are much paler, often straw yellow. These mild beers are light in body and have no distinct hop flavor or aroma. Blonde ales, which are also known as golden ales, are often enjoyed in warmer months because of their light body and drinkability. Due to their relatively low alcohol content, these beers are approachable and won't weigh you down during a hot summer day.

AVERAGE ABV: 4–5%

NOTABLE LOCAL OPTIONS: Cascade Lakes Brewery Blonde Bombshell (Bend, OR), Pyramid Brewing Company Curve Ball (Seattle, WA), Machine House Brewery Golden Ale (Seattle, WA), Postmark Blonde (Vancouver, BC)

GLASSWARE: Tumbler

American Brown Ale

Brewed almost exclusively with brown malts, brown ales, which were first popularized in England, have grown steadily in popularity in America (think: Newcastle Brown Ale). While not as heavy or robust as a porter or stout, brown ales are crisper, often a bit sweet. Flavor notes include caramel and chocolate, though some brown ales are flavored with hazelnut or other ingredients. Brown ales are smooth and incorporate little hops.

AVERAGE ABV: 5–7%

NOTABLE LOCAL OPTIONS: Rogue Ales Hazelnut Brown Nectar (Ashland, OR), Georgetown Brewing Company Bob's Brown Ale (Seattle, WA), Monkey 9 Brewing James Brown Ale (Richmond, BC)

GLASSWARE: Tumbler

American Cream Ale

Despite the name, these beers don't contain any actual dairy. However, they drink creamy and light. Functionally, cream ales are a lot like blonde Guinness stouts. Both are often poured through special nitrogen taps, which gives the beer a smoother texture as a result of the smaller and higher quantity of air bubbles during carbonation. American cream ales, however, are pale gold or straw in color and taste mild in every respect. Lately some craft brewers have started to experiment with hoppy or imperial cream ales, but this is still rare.

AVERAGE ABV: 4–5.5%

NOTABLE LOCAL OPTIONS: McMenamins Moo Moo Meadows Cream Ale on Nitro (Portland, OR), Full Sail Brewing Company Session Cream (Hood River, OR), Hale's Ales Cream Ale (Seattle, WA)

GLASSWARE: Tumbler

American Pale Ale

The American pale ale is the basis for much of what modern craft beer has become. The first popular versions are often attributed to California's Sierra Nevada Brewing and Anchor Brewing, which arrived on the scene in the late 1970s. Both beers, brewed with pale malts, have a bright orange hue and offer a crisp, though hoppy ale. Today this style is popular throughout the country—and especially in the Northwest—for its medium body, pleasant hue, and citrusy aroma.

AVERAGE ABV: 4.5–6.5%

NOTABLE LOCAL OPTIONS: Boneyard Beer Bone-A-Fide (Bend, OR), Deschutes Brewery Mirror Pond Pale Ale (Bend, OR), Georgetown Brewing Company Manny's Pale Ale (Seattle, WA), Granville Island Brewery English Bay Pale Ale (Vancouver, BC)

GLASSWARE: Tumbler

American Wild Ale

American made but Belgian influenced, these sour ales are concocted by introducing a great deal of wild or errant yeasts to the brew by either aging the beer in oak barrels or by simply adding wild yeasts by hand. The result is an acidic, sour beer with a range of flavors due to the range of yeasts and how they are added. Fruity lambics, which are commonly found in Northwest bottle shops and bars, are specific wild ales made with spontaneously fermenting yeast native to Belgium. If you're the sour beer aficionado of your group, you'll want to check out the goses on page 52 too.

AVERAGE ABV: 5–12%

NOTABLE LOCAL OPTIONS: Cascade Brewing Apricot Ale and Vlad the Imp Aler (Portland, OR), de Garde Brewing The Purple (Tillamook, OR), Reuben's Brews Brettania (Seattle, WA), Floating Bridge Brewing Peach Sour (Seattle, WA), Urban Family Tropic Heart (Seattle, WA)

GLASSWARE: Tulip

Barleywine

Named for its high alcohol content, which approaches that of actual wine, barleywine generally come in two styles. American barleywines are hoppier and amber in color while older British varieties are maltier and often darker in hue. Both, however, are big, fruity, and flavorful. Barleywines, which are aged months, are often released in the winter during the chilliest months. Those made with a preponderance of wheat grains are called wheatwines.

———————————————————

AVERAGE ABV: 7–15%

NOTABLE LOCAL OPTIONS: Pelican Brewing Company Mother of All Storms (Pacific City, OR), XZ Old Crustacean (Ashland, OR), Full Sail Brewing Company Old Boardhead (Hood River, OR), Fremont Brewing Brew 3000 (Seattle, WA), Pike Brewing Company Old Bawdy Barley Wine (Seattle, WA)

GLASSWARE: Snifter

Cascadian Dark Ale

These hybrid brews are also known as black IPAs. Cascadian dark ales are made with dark roasted malts and quite a bit of hops. As a result these beers have a dark, often black hue and taste chocolaty and caramelly like a stout and floral or bitter like a West Coast-style IPA.

AVERAGE ABV: 6–9%

NOTABLE LOCAL OPTIONS: Deschutes Brewery Hop in the Dark (Bend, OR), Widmer Brothers Brewing Pitch Black IPA (Portland, OR), Rogue Ales Morimoto Black Obi Soba Ale (Ashland, OR), Pike Brewing Company Octopus Ink Black IPA (Seattle, WA)

GLASSWARE: Tulip

ESB

Short for either extra special bitter or English strong bitter, the ESB is a version of the esoteric bitter ale, which is a name for hoppy English pale ales. While "bitter" is a relic of beer vernacular, the ESB name resurfaces regularly enough in pubs that it's worth noting. ESBs, which experienced resurgence in the Northwest with Redhook's version, are copper-hued, low in carbonation and mildly hoppy and malty. It's a muted pale ale for a British happy hour.

AVERAGE ABV: 4.5–6%

NOTABLE LOCAL OPTIONS: Deschutes Brewery Bachelor ESB (Bend, OR), Redhook Brewery ESB (Seattle, WA), Elysian Brewing Company The Wise ESB (Seattle, WA), Driftwood Brewery Naughty Hildegard ESB (Victoria, BC)

GLASSWARE: Tumbler

Flanders Red Ale

Sadly, this has nothing to do with Homer Simpson's neighbor. Instead, Flanders is an area of Belgium where this sour beer originates. Sour beers are brews made with extra yeast, creating an extra acidic or tart flavor. Flanders red ale, in particular, is a nuanced sour and fruity beer that finishes dry. Red or amber in hue, these beers are barrel-aged over a long period (often longer than a year) and made by blending old and new beers.

AVERAGE ABV: 4–7%

NOTABLE LOCAL OPTIONS: Cascade Brewing Kriek (Portland, OR), Hair of the Dog Brewing Company Michael (Portland, OR), Crux [BANISHED] Better Off Red (Bend, OR), pFriem Family Brewers Flanders Red (Hood River, OR), Georgetown Brewing Company Tom Flanders (Seattle, WA)

GLASSWARE: Tulip

India Pale Ale

In the Northwest just about every brewery feels the need to have their own distinct IPA. Some even have several IPAs in rotation at a given time. IPAs, which are big, strong, and hoppy beers, were invented in the nineteenth century when suds were shipped from the United Kingdom to the British colonies in India. Extra hops were needed for the beers going abroad to help preserve them on the journey. Ever since, the beer has become popular worldwide. Because of the plethora of hops in the Northwest, local IPAs are hoppy to the extreme, while East Coast and British IPAs are often maltier and more medium-bodied. Imperial IPAs, often called double (or even triple) IPAs, are hoppier still and stronger, ranging from 8-12% ABV.

AVERAGE ABV: 5.5–7.5%

NOTABLE LOCAL OPTIONS: Deschutes Brewery Fresh-Squeezed IPA (Bend, OR), Breakside Brewery IPA (Portland, OR), Bale Breaker Brewing Company Topcutter IPA (Yakima Valley, WA), Backroads Brewing Company Freshly Squeezed Juicy IPA (Vancouver, BC)

GLASSWARE: Tulip, tumbler

Irish Red Ale

Similar to the malty Scotch ale, Irish red ales often taste caramelly, malty, and low in hops. They're ruby in color and low in carbonation. Some Irish red ales—like Smithwick's famous version—are named because the suds originated in Ireland and, as you might expect, boast a brilliant red color. When speaking of Irish red ales brewed in the US, however, the lines can get a bit blurry between an Irish red ale recipe and an American amber. Nevertheless, with any of these options, you can't go wrong.

***

AVERAGE ABV: 5–6.5%

NOTABLE LOCAL OPTIONS: Alameda Brewhouse St. Brigid Irish Red (Portland, OR), Old Town Brewing Paulie's Not Irish (Portland, OR), Silver City Brewery Ridgetop Red Ale (Bremerton, WA), Sooke Oceanside Brewery Renfrew Red Ale (Sooke, BC)

GLASSWARE: Nonic

Pumpkin Ale

In the age of the early American colonies, pumpkin ale was the dominant form of beer. Not because it was the best tasting, but because the orange gourds were the most readily available to the settlers. Today pumpkin ale often does not refer to beer made with pumpkin, per se. Rather, it's often pumpkin spiced with cinnamon and other traditional fall flavors around Halloween.

AVERAGE ABV: 4–12%

NOTABLE LOCAL OPTIONS: Rogue Ales Pumpkin Patch Ale (Ashland, OR), Elysian Brewing Company Night Owl Pumpkin Ale and The Great Pumpkin (Seattle, WA), Steamworks Brewing Company Pumpkin Ale (Vancouver, BC)

GLASSWARE: Tulip

Rye Beer

Rye beer is any that is made with specialty rye malt instead of barley. Generally, beers made with rye are darker and taste more roasted. Both ales and lagers can be made with rye malts. More recently the use of rye in brewing has become popular, with brewers making standout darker rye IPAs and rye stouts, for example. While this type of beer can span many styles, it's included in this section because you're most likely to see this type of process used on ales— but don't let that stop you from trying them all!

AVERAGE ABV: 4–8%

NOTABLE LOCAL OPTIONS: Upright Brewing Company Six (#6) (Portland, OR), Reuben's Brews Imperial Rye IPA (Seattle, WA), Flying Lion Brewing Rye Stout (Seattle, WA), Vancouver Island Brewing Royston Rye IPA (Vancouver, BC)

GLASSWARE: Tumbler

Saison

Picture, if you will: Barrels of beer fermenting in the corner of a French barn. Maybe the recipe isn't perfect, maybe there is a mash-up of grains and a few yeast strains (some coming from the errant air). Named after the *season* in which it's often served (summer), these saisons, or farmhouse ales, range from tan to red in color. Saisons are often light, grassy, highly carbonated, and mildly spicy. They're an amalgamation of ingredients, beer meant for the end of the day laborer's shift.

AVERAGE ABV: 4.5–8%

NOTABLE LOCAL OPTIONS: Mazama Saison d'Etre (Corvallis, OR), Fremont Brewing Harvest Ale (Seattle, WA), Holy Mountain Brewing Demonteller (Seattle, WA), Farmstrong Brewing Fiery Saison (Mount Vernon, WA)

GLASSWARE: Tulip

Scotch Ale

The term *Scotch ale* has two connotations. Initially the name meant any full-bodied ale from Scotland. They were often red or amber in color, malty and caramelly, and brewed without much hops. Later, in France and other countries, ales were brewed in peat-smoked barrels and tasted similar to Scotch, the spirit. Scotch ales, therefore, are also smoky amber-colored beers that are more bitter than sweet. Today if you order Scotch ale, it will typically be a hybrid of the two.

AVERAGE ABV: 6–9%

NOTABLE LOCAL OPTIONS: Pike Brewing Company Kilt Lifter (Seattle, WA), Silver City Brewery Big Magnificent Bastard Scotch Ale (Bremerton, WA), Parallel 49 Brewing Salty Scot (Vancouver, BC)

GLASSWARE: Tulip, thistle

Steam Beer

Traditional steam beer used special lager yeasts that fermented at warmer ale temperatures to produce a light, slightly fruity brew. Steam beer, which is also known as California common, was cheap and made without the use of rare and expensive refrigeration. As a result, brewers pumped the stuff to containers on their roofs where steam would form in the cool pacific air. Today many breweries make brews by the same name, but they are more like a standard amber lager—such as San Francisco's Anchor Brewing Company, which trademarked the term *steam beer*.

AVERAGE ABV: 4–6%

NOTABLE LOCAL OPTIONS: Widmer Brothers Brewing Columbia Common Spring Ale (Portland, OR), Pike Brewing Company Derby Lager (Seattle, WA), 33 Acres Brewing 33 Acres of Life (Vancouver, BC)

GLASSWARE: Tumbler

Tripel

Tripel is a word used to describe strong pale ales, or beers that have triple the ingredients. The name first appeared in the historic Westmalle Brewery in the 1930s, and the company still produces them today, along with signature wide-mouthed chalices. Because of its mass of ingredients, the bright yellow beer is strong, fruity, and offers a thick, creamy head. An even stronger version of this recipe is called a quadrupel, and a dubbel is a milder, maltier option.

AVERAGE ABV: 8–12%

NOTABLE LOCAL OPTIONS: Deschutes Brewery SuperBier Trippel (Bend, OR), West Seattle Brewing Company Tripel (Seattle, WA), Triple R Brewery Orange Crunch Tripel (Seattle, WA), Pike Brewing Company Monk's Uncle Tripel (Seattle, WA)

GLASSWARE: Goblet, chalice

Winter Warmer

These are made for the colder months, perfect for drinking by a fireside. Winter warmers, which are dark in color, offer a full body and strong, malty flavor. Sometimes barrel aged, American winter warmers can include spices, such as cinnamon, ginger, or nutmeg. These are known as Christmas ales and are more amber in color. Winter warmers, which have a low hop content but a high alcohol content, are best enjoyed in moderate doses as the snow falls.

AVERAGE ABV: 5.5–12%

NOTABLE LOCAL OPTIONS: Widmer Brothers Brewing Barrel-Aged Brrrbon (Portland, OR), Maritime Pacific Brewing Company Jolly Roger Christmas Ale (Seattle, WA), Redhook Brewery Winterhook (Seattle, WA), Fremont Brewing B-Bomb (Seattle, WA)

GLASSWARE: Goblet, chalice

Cicerone

What Is a Cicerone?

In each essential field, experts are needed. World languages need their professors, biology needs its scientists, and politics needs politicians. In the long, storied history of wine, the role of the expert is filled by sommeliers. In the long, storied history of beer, it's cicerones who fill that role. And while beer experts come in many forms—from home brewer to brewery owner—the cicerone plays a vital role.

Longtime brewer Ray Daniels created the official cicerone certification program in 2008. It has four levels: Certified Beer Server, Certified Cicerone, Advanced Cicerone, and Master Cicerone. The program, which is geared toward improving the standards of beer care, focuses on beer-tending, retail, distribution, and brewing. To many, the cicerone is the steward of craft beer. A cicerone is studied in all facets, from pouring to storage.

"A brewer's biggest fear is to make great beer and then it's not taken care of," says Robyn Schumacher, Seattle's Stoup Brewing cofounder and Washington State's first-ever female cicerone. "Cicerones help to bridge that gap."

To become a cicerone, one has to answer some 150 questions—including long essays—about the history and components of beer. Questions may include, "How is corn or rice generally treated before being mixed with the rest of the malt used in the brewhouse?" (Answer: before mashing, corn and rice are cooked to gelatinize their starches) or "Crystal and chocolate are names for two examples of what ingredient?" (Answer: malts). And while there are only one or two dozen Master Cicerones today, that number will surely increase in the coming years as restaurateurs, retailers, and consumers alike seek high-level understanding and analysis of this vibrant field.

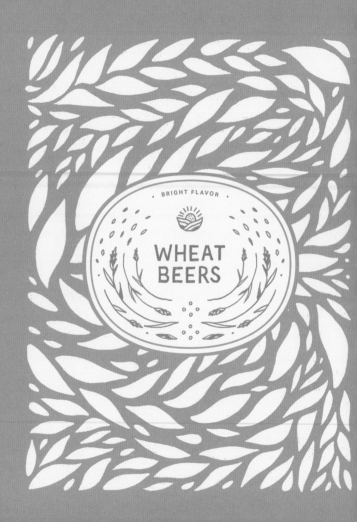

BRIGHT FLAVOR

WHEAT
BEERS

Wheat beers are brewed with ale yeasts at warm temperatures with a majority of wheat instead of barley. As a result they often have a fluffier mouthfeel and brighter flavor. Historically there are two varieties of wheat beers, German and Belgian, distinguished by the fact that many Belgian wheat beers include spices such as coriander and orange peel. In general, most wheat beers are light in color, ranging from white to yellow straw. Though there are several varieties of dark and high-alcohol wheat beers, which we will discuss.

Belgian Witbier

Literally translating to "white beer," the Belgian witbier is unfiltered and hazy. It drinks light and smooth with a touch of spice. Often these beers are served with lemon or orange slices, but traditionalists will tell you to enjoy it without fruit for its full flavor. With the rise of Hoegaarden, Shock Top, and Blue Moon, this style has become more and more popular in the United States.

AVERAGE ABV: 4–7%

NOTABLE LOCAL OPTIONS: Rogue Ales Half-E-Weizen (Ashland, OR), Holy Mountain Brewing White Lodge Belgian-Style White Ale (Seattle, WA), Ghostfish Brewing Company Shrouded Summit Belgian White Ale (Seattle, WA), Driftwood Brewery White Bark Ale (Victoria, BC)

GLASSWARE: Tulip, weizen glass

Dunkelweizen

These are darker (*dunkel* translates to "dark"), maltier hefeweizens. These beers range from an amber to brown color and can share the same clove or banana flavor as their more golden cousins. Dunkelweizen beer, however, always offers a more complex malt character than hefeweizens, and as a result can even be enjoyed after dinner similar to a dessert beer.

AVERAGE ABV: 4–7%

NOTABLE LOCAL OPTIONS: Occidental Brewing Company Dunkelweizen (Portland, OR), Stoup Brewing Dunkelweizen (Seattle, WA), Fish Brewing Company Leavenworth Boulder Bend Dunkelweizen (Olympia, WA)

GLASSWARE: Tulip, weizen glass

German Hefeweizen

Where Belgian witbiers are generally white, German hefeweizens are often a more golden. Hefeweizens are made with little to no hops and a near fifty-fifty balance of wheat to barley, though in more recent iterations the percentage of wheat included in many American hefeweizens has grown. While light in color and body, hefeweizens are unfiltered and, as a result, fluffy and cloudy. The particular yeast used to ferment these beers can create a slight clove or even banana flavor.

AVERAGE ABV: 4–7%

NOTABLE LOCAL OPTIONS: Widmer Brothers Brewing Hefeweizen (Portland, OR), Pyramid Brewing Company Hefeweizen (Seattle, WA), Stoup Brewing Bavarian Hefeweizen (Seattle, WA), Driftwood Brewery Entangled Hopfenweisse (Victoria, BC)

GLASSWARE: Tulip, weizen glass

Gose

A wheat-dominant beer fortified by a wide range of salt, spices, and herbs give this tart and sour beer its distinct flavor. Hazy and light in color, the beer, though generally low in hops, offers salty and floral flavor notes, as well as touches of lemon and coriander. In many ways these are summer beers, to be enjoyed cold in the hot sun. For those especially drawn to sour beers, don't miss the American wild ales on page 27.

AVERAGE ABV: 4–5%

NOTABLE LOCAL OPTIONS: Widmer Brothers Brewing Marionberry Hibiscus Gose (Portland, OR), Holy Mountain Brewing Gose (Seattle, WA), Strange Fellows Brewing Botanik Gin Gose (Vancouver, BC)

GLASSWARE: Pokal, pilsner glass

What Is a Bottle Shop?

Bars and public houses offer neighborhood spots where locals can gather to grab a pint, a bite, and a conversation. But they also have their limitations. Most bars can't offer carryout, meaning patrons can't take bottles or cans home. The beer has to stay on-site at all times. Despite their best efforts, bars can also only offer so many craft options. With rare exception, most bars offer customers no more than one or two dozen varieties from which to choose.

But what about those beer lovers who want more than just the IPA du jour or the everyday lager? In cities like Seattle and Portland, that's where bottle shops come in. While bars and breweries do their best to offer a wide selection of options to their patrons, none can compare to the bounty of a well-stocked bottle shop. Even the deepest tap list can't stand up to a shop like Seattle's Bottleworks, which boasts both multiple locations around the city and upwards of one thousand options from all over the world in each store at any given time.

And about 200 miles south of Seattle, in Portland, Belmont Station offers a similar wide selection, with more than one thousand different beers and ciders available. Cascade Lake Brewery Pineapple Kush IPA? Got it. Finnriver Farm and Cidery Chai Spice Brandywine? Yup. Want to try an authentic beer from England, Germany, or Belgium? Paper or plastic bag? Craft connoisseurs and novice beer drinkers alike can find their favorite standby or something new and exciting to whet their whistles. Bottle shops are community hubs. They offer wall-to-wall options, beer events, tastings, and even educational services about brews from all around the world.

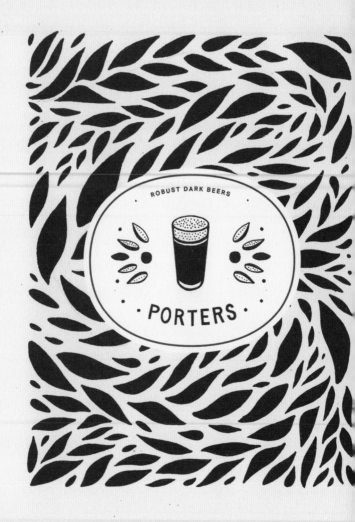

ROBUST DARK BEERS

· PORTERS ·

Porters are robust dark beers that rose to popularity in England during the industrial revolution. They came to be named after the British who carried the heavy beer barrels from brewery to pub. Today the beer style is brewed with ale yeast and pale malts in combination with black, chocolate, crystal, or smoked brown malts. As the popularity of porters rose in Britain, different versions of the beer were made. Extra-strong porters were initially called stout porters; later they were just called stouts. Like porters, stouts often taste roasted or chocolaty. With the rise of home-brewing and craft beer, though, new porter and stout styles have been created, some of which we will investigate here.

American Porter

In many ways the American porter is like a blank slate. Its dark, roasted flavor allows for much experimentation, so porters, by nature, are forgiving beers. As a result brewers have enjoyed creating a multitude of these dark, sumptuous brews. Beer drinkers can enjoy versions such as vanilla porters, mocha porters, coconut porters, raspberry porters, and many more. Or, the standard, a dark, rich pint meant for 5 p.m. that somehow tastes best on a dreary day.

AVERAGE ABV: 5–7%

NOTABLE LOCAL OPTIONS: Deschutes Brewery Black Butte Porter (Bend, OR), Georgetown Brewing Company 9 LB Porter (Seattle, WA), Black Raven Brewing Coco Jones Coconut Porter (Redmond, WA), Vancouver Island Brewing Nanaimo Bar Porter (Vancouver, BC)

GLASSWARE: Tumbler

American Stout

Stouts are generally darker, stronger, *stouter* versions of porters. Big, bold, roasted dark malts blend with copious amounts of American hops to create an unparalleled beer. The combination of the hops and malts creates a balanced cornucopia of flavors and aromas. Want more? Imperial stouts pack an even bigger punch. Pitch-black and upwards of 12% ABV, these beers are meant as proverbial personal heaters for chilling Dostoevsky-era Siberian winters.

AVERAGE ABV: 5.5–9%

NOTABLE LOCAL OPTIONS: Rogue Ales Chocolate Stout (Ashland, OR), Lucky Envelope Brewing Peanut Butter Cream Stout (Seattle, WA), Elysian Brewing Company Dark o' the Moon Pumpkin Stout (Seattle, WA), Storm Brewing Black Plague Stout (Vancouver, BC)

GLASSWARE: Tumbler

Irish Stout

Also known as dry stouts, these beers are often served using a nitrogen gas tap. As a result, similar to American cream ales (see page 25), Irish stouts are smooth, if not moderately fluffy to the palate (think: Guinness). And like American stouts, Irish stouts are dark in color and taste roasted, if not a touch chocolaty.

AVERAGE ABV: 3–7%

NOTABLE LOCAL OPTIONS: Deschutes Brewery Nitro Irish Stout (Bend, OR), Floating Bridge Brewing Dry Stout (Seattle, WA), Persephone Brewing Dry Irish Stout (Gibsons, BC)

GLASSWARE: Nonic

Milk Stout

These beers are brewed with lactose sugars and as a result are sweeter and creamier than average American stouts (see page 61). Also known as cream stouts, these varieties are sweeter than traditional stouts while still maintaining the signature roasted qualities of their other stout brethren. If you're lactose intolerant, this beer is not for you, unfortunately.

AVERAGE ABV: 3–10%

NOTABLE LOCAL OPTIONS: Widmer Brothers Brewing Snow Plow Milk Stout (Portland, OR), Natian Brewery Cease & Desist Milk Stout (Portland, OR), Elysian Brewing Company Split Shot Espresso Milk Stout (Seattle, WA), Hearthstone Brewery Chocolate Milk Stout (North Vancouver, BC)

GLASSWARE: Nonic

Oatmeal Stout

These beers are brewed with oatmeal, the oils from which add a particular smoothness to the beer. Just like traditional American stouts (see page 61), oatmeal stouts are dark, usually pitch-black, and have a distinct roasted or chocolaty malt flavor to go along with their signature silkiness.

AVERAGE ABV: 4–8%

NOTABLE LOCAL OPTIONS: Ninkasi Brewing Oatis and Vanilla Oatis (Eugene, OR), Fremont Brewing Bourbon Barrel-Aged Dark Star (Seattle, WA), Elysian Brewing Company Dragonstooth Stout (Seattle, WA)

GLASSWARE: Nonic

a
plant-based beverage

Ⓥ

GF

What Is Vegan Beer?

Today most beers are vegan. Whether we're talking big names like Budweiser in America, Heineken in Holland, or Tsingtao in China, the vast majority of beers are not made with any animal products. But that hasn't always been the case. Historically, some beers were filtered with animal parts, which were often either sticky fish intestines or gluey gelatins that captured errant floating particles in the suds. And some beers, such as Australia's Foster's, still haven't gone full vegan.

Today, however, as the process became more technologically advanced and with the rise of vegan and vegetarian diets, the vast majority of breweries no longer use those techniques. Outside of arcane tradition, there is no longer any essential use for animal parts in the beer-making process. While some do continue to use animal by-products, as the times continue to change, more efforts are being made to spruce up the suds we drink.

In Seattle, Elliott Bay Brewing Company has gone both completely vegan *and* certified organic. To be officially organic, the USDA must examine a brewery's equipment and ingredients for compliance. It can be both an arduous and expensive process, but the designation can be extremely important to brewers, farmers, and customers. And while not every brewery can keep its brewing processes vegan or organic, many do.

Gluten-free beer is another request in Northwest bars. So is nonalcoholic beer. But both are quite difficult to produce. It can be costly to dedicate an entire section of a brewery to specialty beer. Gluten-free beer, which is made without traditional barleys, wheat, and other grains, and nonalcoholic beer, which is made by brewing beer and then removing the alcohol, often don't have enough of a popular draw to make the production profitable to companies without deep pockets. But with enough demand that could change, as we see breweries like Omission in Portland and Ghostfish Brewing Company in Seattle dedicating their entire production to gluten-free offerings.

Today when most think of lagers, they often think of cheap options like Budweiser. But there is in fact a wide range of lagers, from light and easy drinking to dark and heavy. In broad terms, lagers differ from all other beers in one major area: they are cold conditioned (gradually cooled to near freezing to achieve greater clarity) and done so over longer periods using *Saccharomyces pastorianus* yeast. Ales, on the other hand, are fermented in warmer temperatures for often only a week or two. Lagers, as a result, end up drinking cleaner, clearer, and less fruity than their ale counterparts. The process, which was invented hundreds of years ago, became more popular in the nineteenth century. In the Czech Republic, brewers would "lager" their beers in caves during the summer months to condition it cold prior to the invention of refrigeration.

Altbier

Something of a hybrid, altbier is made with ale yeast at warm temperatures but conditioned longer and cold like a lager. As a result the style loses some of the fruity notes that one- or two-week-old ales offer after short periods of fermentation. Altbier is an old German style. *Alt* translates to "old," a nod to how long the beer is stored before drinking and how old the recipe is. Formerly considered a German-style brown ale, altbier is officially today considered a dark lager.

AVERAGE ABV: 4–7%

NOTABLE LOCAL OPTIONS: Ninkasi Brewing Company Sleigh'r Dark Doüble Alt Ale (Eugene, OR), Widmer Brothers Brewing Okto Festival Ale (Portland, OR), Georgetown Brewing Company Shultzy's (Seattle, WA), Driftwood Brewery Crooked Coast Altbier (Victoria, BC)

GLASSWARE: Stange, pokal

American Amber Lager

While lagers today are commonly thought of as both light in body and hue, lagers originally were darker beers with richer, more complex flavors. Similar to American amber ales (see page 22), amber lagers can range in flavor and color, from light and crisp to darker, maltier, and heavier. Generally, American amber lagers taste lightly hopped, toasted, and a touch like caramel. Other regions around the world pride themselves on their darker, nuanced lagers, including the chocolaty and nutty Munich dunkel lagers and crisp, roasted Vienna lagers.

AVERAGE ABV: 4.5–6%

NOTABLE LOCAL OPTIONS: pFriem Family Brewers Vienna Lager (Hood River, OR), Full Sail Brewing Company Session Fest (Hood River, OR), Chuckanut Brewery Vienna Lager (Bellingham, WA), Vancouver Island Brewing Storm Watcher Winter Lager (Vancouver, BC)

GLASSWARE: Pilsner glass, pokal, tumbler

American Lager

American lagers are light, clear, and often straw-yellow beers brewed with plentiful carbonation. American lagers are not hoppy or malty; instead their mellow, neutral qualities are the draw. Craft American lagers can offer stronger flavor notes than their domestic American adjunct lager brands like Budweiser. American lagers often taste toasted, with mild biscuit- or bread-like aromas.

AVERAGE ABV: 4–5%

NOTABLE LOCAL OPTIONS: Portland Brewing Company Portland Lager (Portland, OR), Maritime Pacific Brewing Company Old Seattle Lager (Seattle, WA), Steamworks Brewing Company Lion's Gate Lager (Vancouver, BC)

GLASSWARE: Pilsner glass, pokal, tumbler

German Bock

These high-octane lagers have a long and fruitful relationship with their home country of Germany. So popular were bocks that the style branched off into several popular subsections. Traditionally, German bocks were strong, dark, and malty and brewed without much hops. Today bocks can range from a light copper in color to a dark chocolate brown. Doppelbocks are stronger versions (8–11% ABV) and often sweeter than traditional bocks. Monks originally drank these during times of fasting. Maibocks are beers brewed with the lighter helles lager (see page 76) recipe but made to bock ABV strength. Eisbock are doppelbocks that are partially frozen with the excess water removed, increasing the flavor and the alcohol content (8–14% ABV).

AVERAGE ABV: 6–8%

NOTABLE LOCAL OPTIONS: Rogue Ales Dead Guy Maibock (Ashland, OR), Chuckanut Brewery Doppelbock (Bellingham, WA), Pyramid Brewing Honey Bock (Seattle, WA), Vancouver Island Brewing Hermannator Eisbock (Vancouver, BC)

GLASSWARE: Tulip, snifter, chalice, goblet

Helles Lager

Bright, pale lagers, the helles style doesn't veer far from modern pilsners. Helles lagers are often golden in color, mildly sweet, with moderate hops. Helles lagers are a bit sturdier than average straw-colored pilsners, and until recently the style was largely only prominent in southern Germany. Now, though, craft brewers have enjoyed producing some helles lagers locally with the rise of more craft beer experimentation.

AVERAGE ABV: 4.5–5.5%

NOTABLE LOCAL OPTIONS: Ninkasi Brewing Helles Belles (Eugene, OR), Pike Brewing Company King of Cascadia Helles (Seattle, WA), Fremont Brewing Helles Lager (Seattle, WA), Coal Harbour Brewing Company 311 Helles Lager (Vancouver, BC)

GLASSWARE: Flute, tumbler

Kölsch

The recipe for kölsch is specific. The beer, which is fermented at warm temperatures like ale but stored in cold conditions like lager, is hoppy, bright, and well filtered so that it remains clear. As a result kölsch drinks like a crisp pale ale, lighter in body than an American pale ale or IPA but with more herbal hop notes than a lager. And while many may confuse it for an ale, a kölsch is formally a lager.

AVERAGE ABV: 4–6%

NOTABLE LOCAL OPTIONS: Breakside Brewery Kölsch (Portland, OR), Occidental Brewing Company Kölsch (Portland, OR), Chuckanut Brewery Kölsch (Bellingham, WA), Georgetown Brewing Company L.A. Woman Crystal Kölsch (Seattle, WA)

GLASSWARE: Stange, pokal

Oktoberfest

While most associate the word *Oktoberfest* with a German beer festival, fewer know the origins of the festival are rooted in a type of beer. Before Maytag and Sears, when refrigeration was impossible, German brewers would make a cold-conditioned beer they would store underground in caves in the summer months. In the fall—around October—they would drink the beer to celebrate their patience and prepare for winter. Oktoberfest (a.k.a. *Marzen*, for March, the month they're brewed) beers are often copper in color, malty, and rich with little to no hop presence.

AVERAGE ABV: 5–6.5%

NOTABLE LOCAL OPTIONS: Portland Brewing Company Uncle Otto's Octoberfest Marzen (Portland, OR), Chuckanut Brewery Old Fest (Bellingham, WA), Red Collar Brewing Marzen (Vancouver, BC)

GLASSWARE: Seidel, stein, tankard, boot

Pilsner

As brewers began experimenting with cool fermenting yeasts and conditioning their beers in cold temperatures, new styles arose, like the lager. But in 1842, in the city of Pilsen, brewers came up with a new style, the pale lager, or the pilsner. Named after the city in which it originated, pilsners (a.k.a. Bohemian pilsners) were sweeter, slightly darker, and toastier than most pilsners we drink today. Modern pilsners are most often lighter and pale yellow to straw in color. American imperial pilsners are hoppier and stronger, ranging from 7–9% ABV.

AVERAGE ABV: 4–5.5%

NOTABLE LOCAL OPTIONS: Chuckanut Brewery Pilsner Lager (Bellingham, WA), pFriem Family Brewers Pilsner (Hood River, OR), Vancouver Island Bohemian Pilsner (Vancouver, BC)

GLASSWARE: Pilsner glass, flute

What Is a Beard Beer?

Microbreweries are a lot like laboratories. There are big, sterilized containers full of bubbling liquids. There are white coats and constant dialogue around new experiments. And sometimes those experiments lead to new concoctions that are created and unleashed out into the world. Many of these experiments have yielded tremendous results. Seattle's Cloudburst Brewing, for example, keeps a large roll of butcher block paper hung up behind its cash register because its beer menu rotates so often they have to change it by hand. They move that fast.

But brewing experiments don't always yield the tastiest of treats—how could they? Even Babe Ruth struck out once in a while. So, sometimes what the microbreweries produce must be tossed before it can do any more harm.

Exhibit A: Rogue Ales' Beard Beer. Officially an American wild ale, the Ashland, Oregon, brewery made the stuff using wild yeast from beard hairs plucked from the chin of its former head brewer, John Maier. While the beer enjoyed some critical acclaim—and international news for the oddity of it—the beer has not made the brewery's regular rotation.

Odin Brewing Company in Tukwila, Washington, created a bacon ale with smoked peat malt that didn't last long (and for good reason). Lucky Envelope Brewing in Seattle tried a ramen beer with several bricks of noodles and accompanying flavor packets that never got off the ground. And another Emerald City spot, Floating Bridge Brewing, brewed a salsa beer using tomatoes, cilantro, lime, and jalapeño for Cinco de Mayo. On another occasion, Floating Bridge also tried a rhubarb saison that didn't pass muster.

"The first sips were kind of fun," says Russ Cornell, head brewer at Floating Bridge. "The sour built up on your tongue. But most of that batch went down the drain. We shouldn't imply that we always say 'that's perfect' for the first batch of any new beer though. There's always a way to make a beer better. That's what makes life interesting as a brewer."

BEER GLASSWARE

JUST AS THERE ARE many styles of beer, there are many styles of glassware created to showcase a beer's best qualities. Want to admire the bright straw-yellow color of a hefeweizen? There's a glass specially made for that. Want to sit beside a fire with a glass fit for a royal sip of strong barleywine? There's a particular glass for that too. Here we will investigate all the glassware options, each of which is designed to help you enjoy your favorite beer no matter the style.

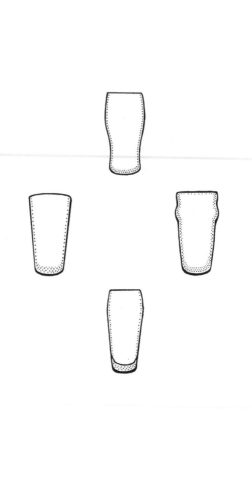

The Pints

Pint glasses are tall, cylindrical, and have a wide mouth (though not as wide a mouth as a chalice or goblet). Pint glasses, which range from 16 to 20 ounces, are the most common beer glasses and are found stacked by the dozens in pubs and bars around the world. There are four types of pint glasses, each defined by subtle design differences and its country of origin.

Irish

This option (also known as the Guinness glass) has an even narrower base and a more bulbous middle. These glasses often hold 20 ounces of beer and are generally reserved for Ireland's signature thick and cascading Guinness stouts.

Nonic

This large English-style pub glass has a narrow base, wide mouth, and a bulge near the top, which helps for extra grip. These glasses hold 20 ounces of beer.

Tumbler

This US-style glass resembles the nonic glass, except that this glass holds 16 ounces, not 20. Some tumblers, however, are simpler. They're conical, straight-edged, without the signature nonic bulge near the top.

Willybecher

This German-style glass looks like a hybrid of a tulip and a stange. The willybecher (or willi becher) has a narrow body, wider center, and a tapered mouth that finishes in a tulip flare. This glass showcases a beer's hue and its tapered, flared mouth helps with retaining the beer's frothy head.

The Delicates

While some glasses are meant for the full-bodied complex stuff, some glassware is made for lighter beers—or, those subtle suds made with minimal ingredients that offer a light body and crisp flavor.

Flute

Slight and elegant, flutes are made to showcase light-colored and light-bodied beer. It's the type of glass you hold to the light by its stem with your thumb and index finger to admire the clarity of a lager. The glass promotes small, deliberate sips and its narrow mouth promotes the beer's subtle aroma and flavor to the top of the glass for focused flavor detection.

Tulip

These flower-shaped stemmed glasses have bulbous bottoms and narrow mouths that flare out like a blossom. The bigger, rounded bottoms enhance beer "volatiles," or the aspects of beer that impact flavor and aroma. As the shape would suggest, tulip glasses, which vary in size, capture and push a beer's aromatics upward so they rise and splay on the palate. While these glasses are common, they look unique amidst the everyday pints and mugs.

Pilsner Glass

Similar to flute glasses, pilsner glasses are made slender to showcase a beer's bright hue and often clear color. Pilsner glasses differ from flutes, though, in that they're taller, wider, without a stem, and are designed less like a teardrop and more like a capitol I. With a weighted base and a mouth that widens subtly to promote carbonation, pilsner glasses are narrow and some, known as footed pilsner glasses, come with a narrower base and round disc-like foot.

Pokal

Otherwise known as stemmed pilsner glasses, European pokals are meant for lighter beers. With a bulbous bottom and tapered mouth, pokals are straight-edged and stylish. The 16-ounce glasses retain a beer's aroma, focusing it toward the drinker's nose before each sip.

Stange

The German word *stange* translates to "stick." The tall, cylindrical stange glasses, therefore, are slender and straight-edged like a hollowed-out glass dowel. Originally, stanges were about 7 ounces, but more recently glassmakers have created bigger 12- and 13-ounce versions to fit the contents of bottled beers. Like pilsner glasses or flutes, a stange's narrow mouth focuses nuanced malt and hop flavors and helps retain a light beer's puffy head.

Weizen Glass

These figure-eight glasses are made exclusively for wheat beers. Tall and shapely, weizen glasses are a hybrid of a pilsner glass and tulip glass. The length and shape of the glass showcases the bright hue of the wheat beer and helps to maintain its feathery head.

The Mugs

These hefty containers have a long, storied history in their native Germany. Whether they are large or small, served chilled or at room temperature, composed of clay, metal, or glass, made with a hinged cap on top or an open mouth—there's almost always a mug appropriate for any beer serving and savoring occasion.

Oktoberfest

Similar to the boot (housed in the Oddities category, page 115), these glasses are comically big, holding as much as 60 ounces. Oktoberfest mug surfaces are often dimpled (similar to seidels) for better grip and have thick glass walls, which insulate the beer and keep it from chipping if it's set down too fast or if a beer drinker gives an overzealous "Cheers!"

Seidel

These glasses are shorter than their Oktoberfest counter-parts. Nevertheless, they're sturdy from handle to glass walls. Seidels are also commonly referred to as dimpled mugs because of the many indented areas on their surface, just like their larger cousins, which aid grip. Seidels, like all mugs, have wide mouths for big, victorious gulps.

Stein

A stein is a large beer mug often made from pewter that includes a hinged lid. The lid, legend has it, was created during the times of the plague to protect from errant and infected flies falling into the brew. Steins, which range from 16 to 32 ounces, are often more ornate and decorated, depicting family crests or a region's local scenery.

Tankard

Likely history's most common beer mug, these plain, straight-edged, thick-walled, often-metal containers are regularly chilled before use. Their sturdy composition makes them useful for celebrating because they're unlikely to crack or break.

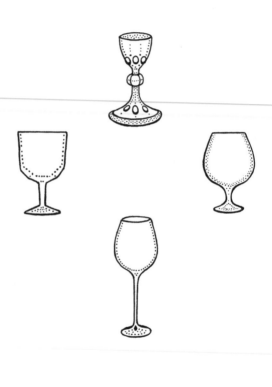

The Regals

Some glassware options simply stand out on their own. Whether it's lavish decoration, tall stems, or the big bowls on top, some options simply scream, "Look at all I can afford!" The following glasses are those opulent options meant to alert your neighbors that you're doing quite well, so no need for the cheap see-through light beers tonight.

Chalice

Everything about the chalice is ornate, from its thick walls to its fat stem and decorative silver and gold trimming. Chalices were made for the wealthy to enjoy their expensive, ingredient-rich beers. You won't find a peasant's pilsner in this glass. Rather, they're for rich beers with flavors that need lots of sensory attention. The chalice's wide mouth allows for the beer drinker to smell the beer's many aromatic notes and take in a large sip to savor the depth of flavors.

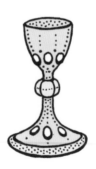

Goblet

Similar in function to the chalice, goblets are more delicate, a bit taller, and bit gawkier. Their stems are longer and their glass walls a bit thinner. While kings and queens drink from chalices, dukes and duchesses drink from the less ornate goblets. Nevertheless, they provide a similar service, show-casing full-bodied, complex beers with their wide mouths.

Oversized Wineglass

If goblets are for dukes, the oversized wineglasses, which are taller than both, are for their interns. These 22-ounce glasses are exactly what they sound like. They have a plain, simple design, a long, thin stem, and a big, bulbous glass with a wide mouth to savor beers like barleywines or dark ales. But they have few of the ornate qualities that distinguish their more refined counterparts.

Snifter

While these glasses vary in size, their purpose always remains the same. Snifters, which are also used for liquors such as cognac and brandy, are meant for swirling liquid—specifically rich, strong beers such as strong ales or imperial stouts. This process "opens up" the flavors by oxygenating the beer and offers warmth from the drinker's hand. Snifters are often stubby, stemmed, and have small mouths that focus the beer's aroma toward the top of the glass.

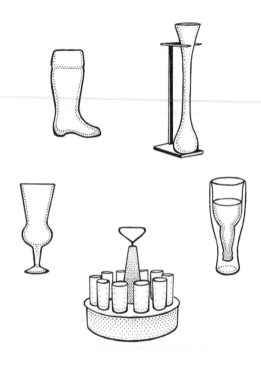

The Oddities

Some beer glasses seem to come from out of nowhere.
Some seem so odd that one wonders how anyone could have
thought them up. Some, well, look like someone was drinking when they were designed. Nevertheless, they all have
their function and place in the greater glassware galaxy.

Boot

According to legend a Prussian general promised his troops to drink from his boot if his men were victorious in an upcoming battle. Not wanting to fulfill his promise literally, the general had a glassmaker fashion a drinking glass into the shape of a boot. Ever since the boot has been a symbol of good luck in Germany and gluttony by US college students. Though boots vary in size, from 12 ounces to multiple liters, it's thought that the bigger the boot, the better for chugging cheap beer.

Hopside Down

These funny-looking beer glasses boast thick walls to provide ultimate beer insulation. The inside of the glass is made in the shape of an upside bottle (thus, the clever name), with the narrowest part of the opening at the bottom surrounded by thick glass. Beers stay cold and the oddity provides a conversation icebreaker.

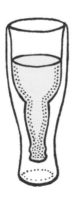

Thistle

These glasses are larger variations on the tulip beer glass. The glass's mouth (or, blossom) flares more dramatically than tulip glasses to resemble Scotland's national flower. Thistles are tall and often range between 15 and 20 ounces. They are used most often to serve strong, malty Scotch ales.

Kranz

While not a piece of glassware, per se, the kranz is capable
of carrying a dozen stanges from tap to table. During busy
times at German bars, servers will utilize these in order
to hold more glasses than they otherwise could with bare
hands. A kranz has a circular base with a 2-inch-tall wall and
a tall handle.

Yard

These tall glasses, measuring at about 3 feet (hence the name), look almost like giant science beakers. They have bulbous bottoms, a long neck, and a wide mouth. Yards can hold 2–3 liters of beer. These glasses often come with wooden stands that secure them safely between sips.

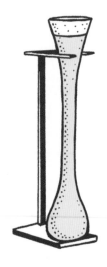

What Is a Crowler?

While the glassware options detailed previously are dedicated to drinking beer at home or in your favorite local pub, there are more vessels dedicated to the transportation of beer so that it can be purchased at one location and enjoyed in another at a later time.

The most widely used beer container is the keg, which comes in various sizes, ranging from a few pints to more than one hundred. While perhaps not relevant in most households, home-bar renovations can incorporate this larger option, or a tub filled with ice makes for easy access for all your summer BBQ needs.

Other common beer containers include aluminum cans and glass bottles, which range from 12 to 16 ounces, all the way up to 40 ounces. Bottles, which are translucent, let in one of beer's two major archenemies: light. Light, along with oxygen, are the elements that make beer go skunky (taste bad) or flat. Most bottles, as a result, are dark green or brown. Opaque cans, however, better protect beer from harmful light.

As the craft revolution has grown in popularity so has the growler: a refillable, 64-ounce glass jug made to carry beer and keep it fresh for a few days in the refrigerator. While growlers were used in the nineteenth century to transport beer from the bar to the home, they've become more ubiquitous in the twenty-first century with the rise of neighborhood tap houses.

But we still haven't answered our opening question! *What is a crowler?* A crowler is a hybrid mix of the can and growler, highlighting the best of both designs. The crowler, which is a 32-ounce sealable metal can, is the newest takeaway option getting more attention and accessibility as our craft scene continues its boom. Crowlers, which don't let in natural light, still allow you to choose from any tap available and can be sealed on site, so your choice of fills is endless. They do require a special machine to adhere the can's top, but if the proper equipment is available, it's often the best and safest way to transport your favorite craft beer.

Resources

Books

While we've worked to provide a crash course on Northwest beer culture in these pages, there are many other great tomes available for those interested in learning more about the variety and history of craft beer in the region and beyond. For those seeking further readings to expand and delve into more suds specifics, we suggest the following.

Beer Pairing: The Essential Guide from the Pairing Pros
by Julia Herz and Gwen Conley

Beyond the Pale: The Story of Sierra Nevada Brewing Co.
by Ken Grossman

Bitter Brew: The Rise and Fall of Anheuser-Busch and America's Kings of Beer
by William Knoedelseder

The Brewer's Tale: A History of the World According to Beer
by William Bostwick

Brewing Revolution: Pioneering the Craft Beer Movement
by Frank Appleton

The Complete Beer Course: Boot Camp for Beer Geeks
by Joshua M. Bernstein

The Craft Beer Cookbook: From IPAs and Bocks to Pilsners and Porters
by Jacquelyn Dodd

Experimental Homebrewing: Mad Science in the Pursuit of Great Beer
by Drew Beechum and Denny Conn

Goodnight Brew: A Parody for Beer People
by Karla Oceanak

How to Brew: Everything You Need to Know to Brew Great Beer Every Time
by John J. Palmer

The New World Guide to Beer
by Michael Jackson (the writer, not the singer)

The Oxford Companion to Beer
by Garrett Oliver

Northwest Festivals

One of the most cherished aspects of craft beer is the community it engenders. After all, *people* are the ones who enjoy the beer, making conversation while sipping their pints, getting to know neighbors at their favorite public houses. Craft beer is often a hearth around which people gather and nowhere is this most evident than at the many Northwest beer festivals throughout the year. These craft-centric events showcase the plethora of pints available and allow beer lovers to meet the folks who make their favorite suds. Following are some of the most popular craft beer festivals in the Northwest.

Washington

BELGIAN FEST: Often held in January, this Seattle-based celebration focuses on the beers from Belgium that have influenced so many modern varieties today.

BREMERTON SUMMER BREWFEST: Often held in July, this festival is a beautiful ferry ride away from the Emerald City in the cozy town of Bremerton.

FREMONT OKTOBERFEST: This October festival celebrates the history of German Oktoberfest beers, in all their shapes and sizes.

THE FRESH HOP ALE FESTIVAL: Often held in October, this Yakima, Washington, gathering celebrates all there is to love about fresh-hop ales.

LEAVENWORTH OKTOBERFEST: Held annually in October in Washington's Little Bavaria (a.k.a. Leavenworth), this beer festival features giant mugs and authentic lederhosen.

SEATTLE INTERNATIONAL BEERFEST: Often held in July, this is a party of worldwide proportions held annually at Seattle Center.

SPOKANE BREWERS FESTIVAL: Often held in May, this celebration on the eastern side of the state highlights breweries in and around the Spokane area.

TRI-CITIES CRAFT BEER FESTIVAL: Often held in April, this festival east of the Cascades celebrates suds hundreds of miles southeast of Seattle proper.

WASHINGTON BREWERS FESTIVAL: Often held in June, this festival focuses on the beers made in Washington State—and there are many!

THE WEST SEATTLE BEER AND MUSIC FESTIVAL: Often held in August, this neighborhood gathering has blossomed into a full-on city block party.

Oregon

BEND BREWFEST: Often held in August, this festival celebrates the best of the best in the small Oregon town.

HOOD RIVER HOPS FEST: Often held in September, this festival highlights the best of local craft beers along with some of the best fresh-hop ales.

IIPA FEST: Often held in August, this festival highlights the hoppy, strong, and floral regional double IPA favorites.

MOUNT ANGEL OKTOBERFEST: Held in the charming town of Mount Angel each September, this festival celebrates the history and varieties of German food and drink.

OREGON BREWERS FESTIVAL: Often held in late July, this Oregon-focused celebration focuses on the suds made in the Beaver State.

PORTLAND CRAFT BEER FESTIVAL: Often held in early July, this City of Roses beer celebration brings family and friends to frolic over mostly locally made brews.

PORTLAND FARMHOUSE AND WILD ALE FESTIVAL: Often held in May, this beer festival celebrates the rustic and complex wild ales, from saisons to sour ales.

PORTLAND FRESH HOPS FESTIVAL: Almost every area brewery is located within 100 miles of a hop farm in Portland and this festival celebrates the beers made as a result of that proximity.

PORTLAND INTERNATIONAL BEERFEST: Often held in June, this citywide beer celebration focuses on the suds made all over the world.

SHEBREW: Often held in March, this beer festival focuses on the often underrepresented population in the brewing world: women.

Vancouver, BC

OKTOBERFEST AT THE VANCOUVER ALPEN CLUB: Put a feather in your cap, tighten your suspenders, and lager the night away with one of the largest selections in the city.

VANCOUVER BREWFEST: Often held in August, this festival is about all things craft—from beer to cider to food and much in between.

WHISTLER VILLAGE BEER FESTIVAL: Come and enjoy some suds where the Olympians also experienced great triumph. Trade ski poles for pint glasses and let the snow tickle your nose with a nice stout pint.

Organizations and Links

AMERICAN HOMEBREWERS ASSOCIATION: A one-stop shop for home-brewing

HOMEBREWERSASSOCIATION.ORG

BEERADVOCATE **MAGAZINE:** The leader in craft beer news

BEERADVOCATE.COM

BEST OF CRAFT BEER AWARDS: A prestigious craft beer awards body

BESTOFCRAFTBEERAWARDS.COM

CRAFT BEER SCRIBE: Dedicated to Oregon and Southwest Washington craft beer news

CRAFTBEERSCRIBE.COM

EXPERIMENTAL BREWING: Dedicated to inventive and exhaustive home-brewing

EXPERIMENTALBREW.COM

FRESH FEST BEER FEST: Dedicated to Black-owned breweries

FRESHFESTBEERFEST.COM

GREAT AMERICAN BEER FESTIVAL: A prestigious American craft beer awards body

GREATAMERICANBEERFESTIVAL.COM

HOMEBREW EXCHANGE: A Portland-based home-brew supply store

HOMEBREWEXCHANGE.NET

NORTHWEST MICROBREWERIES: An active list of Northwest breweries

NORTHWESTMICROBREWERIES.COM

PINK BOOTS SOCIETY: An organization dedicated to women in brewing

PINKBOOTSSOCIETY.ORG

***SIP* MAGAZINE:** A glossy magazine dedicated to Northwest beverages

SIPMAGAZINE.COM

SOUND HOMEBREW SUPPLY: A Seattle-based home-brew supply store

SOUNDHOMEBREW.COM

WASHINGTON BEER BLOG: A blog dedicated to Washington craft beer news

WASHINGTONBEERBLOG.COM

Index

About the Author

JACOB UITTI's work has appeared in the *Washington Post*, *Interview*, *American Songwriter*, *PopMatters*, the *Seattle Times*, and many other publications. When not poring over a keyboard mid-interview, Jake can be found in search of the city's best fried chicken or cheese pizza slice. He is the creator of the TV show *Video Bebop* and author of *Unique Eats and Eateries of Seattle* and *100 Things to Do in Seattle Before You Die* from Reedy Press. The son of Ivy League professors, Jake grew up amid tomes of French literature, but soulful meals, compelling conversation, and thoughtful music are his true loves.

About the Illustrator

JAKE STOUMBOUS is an illustrator, animator, and graphic designer based out of Seattle, Washington. With his roots in studio art and education in graphic design, Jake has a unique approach to creation, working seamlessly between analog and digital media. Jake was born and raised in the Pacific Northwest, where he grew a love for nature, music, and skateboarding. His work is continually inspired by conversation and collaboration with a vibrant community of artists and mentors. To see more of Jake's work, visit his Instagram @stoombz, or find him online at JakeStoumbos.com.